This edition copyright © Robert Frederick Ltd.
Downwood, Claverton Down Road, Bath BA2 6DT

First Published 1994
All rights reserved.

The Bower Meadow by Dante Gabriel Rossetti has been reproduced with kind permission
from Manchester City Art Gallery

Typesetting by Creative Design & Typesetting;
Printed in Malaysia

THE
PRE-RAPHAELITE
BOOK OF
ADDRESSES

Notes & Numbers

Personal Notes

Name ....

Address ....

....

....

Tel.: Home ....

    Business ....

    Car ....

In Case of Emergency

Contact ....

Telephone No. ....

Blood Group ....

Known Allergies ....

Useful Information

eg. Passport Details, Car Information etc

....

....

....

....

....

....

....

....

....

....

....

Notes & Numbers

Useful Telephone Numbers

Accountant ....

Airport ....

Bank ....

Building Society ....

Club ....

Dentist ....

Doctor ....

Electrician ....

Gas ....

Optician ....

Plumber ....

Railway Station ....

Solicitor ....

Taxi/Car Hire ....

Travel Agent ....

Vet ....

Water ....

Others

Dates to Remember

January

....
....
....
....
....
....
....

February

....
....
....
....
....
....
....

March

....
....
....
....
....
....
....

April

....
....
....
....
....
....

May

....
....
....
....
....
....

June

....
....
....
....
....
....

Dates to Remember

July

October

August

November

September

December

'I am Half Sick of Shadows,' said the Lady of Shalott (1915) by John William Waterhouse

A

Name ....
Address ....
....
....
Telephone ....

Name ....
Address ....
....
....
Telephone ....

Name ....
Address ....
....
....
Telephone ....

Name ....
Address ....
....
....
Telephone ....

Name ....
Address ....
....
....
Telephone ....

Name ....

Address ....

....

....

Telephone ....

Name ....

Address ....

....

....

Telephone ....

Name ....

Address ....

....

....

Telephone ....

Name ....

Address ....

....

....

Telephone ....

Name ....

Address ....

....

....

Telephone ....

Name ....

Address ....

....

....

Telephone ....

Name ....

Address ....

....

....

Telephone ....

Name ....

Address ....

....

....

Telephone ....

Name ....

Address ....

....

....

Telephone ....

Name ....

Address ....

....

....

Telephone ....

B

Name ....

Address ....

....

Telephone ....

Name ....

Address ....

....

Telephone ....

Name ....

Address ....

....

Telephone ....

Name ....

Address ....

....

Telephone ....

Name ....

Address ....

....

Telephone ....

La Pia de' Tolomei by Dante Gabriel Rossetti

Name ....

Address ....

....

....

Telephone ....

Name ....

Address ....

....

....

Telephone ....

Name ....

Address ....

....

....

Telephone ....

Name ....

Address ....

....

....

Telephone ....

Name ....

Address ....

....

....

Telephone ....

Name

Address

Telephone

Name

Address

Telephone

Name

Address

Telephone

Name

Address

Telephone

Name

Address

Telephone

C

Name ....
Address ....
....
Telephone ....

Name ....
Address ....
....
Telephone ....

Name ....
Address ....
....
Telephone ....

Name ....
Address ....
....
Telephone ....

Name ....
Address ....
....
Telephone ....

Name ....

Address ....

....

....

Telephone ....

Name ....

Address ....

....

....

Telephone ....

Name ....

Address ....

....

....

Telephone ....

Name ....

Address ....

....

....

Telephone ....

Name ....

Address ....

....

....

Telephone ....

La Belle Dame Sans Merci by John William Waterhouse

C

Name ....

Address ....

....

....

Telephone ....

Name ....

Address ....

....

....

Telephone ....

Name ....

Address ....

....

....

Telephone ....

Name ....

Address ....

....

....

Telephone ....

Name ....

Address ....

....

....

Telephone ....

Name ....

Address ....

....

Telephone ....

Name ....

Address ....

....

Telephone ....

Name ....

Address ....

....

Telephone ....

Name ....

Address ....

....

Telephone ....

Name ....

Address ....

....

....

Telephone ....

Name ....

Address ....

....

....

Telephone ....

Name ....

Address ....

....

....

Telephone ....

Name ....

Address ....

....

....

Telephone ....

Name ....

Address ....

....

....

Telephone ....

Name ....

Address ....

....

....

Telephone ....

Name ....

Address ....

....

....

Telephone ....

Name ....

Address ....

....

....

Telephone ....

Name ....

Address ....

....

....

Telephone ....

Name ....

Address ....

....

....

Telephone ....

Name ....

Address ....

....

....

Telephone ....

April Love by Arthur Hughes

E

Name ....
Address ....
....
Telephone ....

Name ....
Address ....
....
Telephone ....

Name ....
Address ....
....
Telephone ....

Name ....
Address ....
....
Telephone ....

Name ....
Address ....
....
Telephone ....

Name ....
Address ....
....
....
Telephone ....

Name ....
Address ....
....
....
Telephone ....

Name ....
Address ....
....
....
Telephone ....

Name ....
Address ....
....
....
Telephone ....

Name ....
Address ....
....
....
Telephone ....

E

Name ....

Address ....

....

....

Telephone ....

Name ....

Address ....

....

....

Telephone ....

Name ....

Address ....

....

....

Telephone ....

Name ....

Address ....

....

....

Telephone ....

Name ....

Address ....

....

....

Telephone ....

Name ....

Address ....

....

....

Telephone ....

Name ....

Address ....

....

....

Telephone ....

Name ....

Address ....

....

....

Telephone ....

Name ....

Address ....

....

....

Telephone ....

Name ....

Address ....

....

....

Telephone ....

Isabella and the Pot of Basil by William Holman Hunt

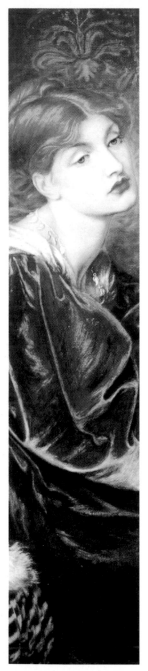

$\mathcal{F}$

Name ....
Address ....
....
....
Telephone ....

Name ....
Address ....
....
....
Telephone ....

Name ....
Address ....
....
....
Telephone ....

Name ....
Address ....
....
....
Telephone ....

Name ....
Address ....
....
....
Telephone ....

F

Name ....

Address ....

....

....

Telephone ....

Name ....

Address ....

....

....

Telephone ....

Name ....

Address ....

....

....

Telephone ....

Name ....

Address ....

....

....

Telephone ....

Name ....

Address ....

....

....

Telephone ....

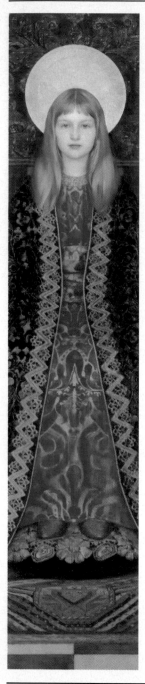

Name ....

Address ....

....

....

Telephone ....

Name ....

Address ....

....

....

Telephone ....

Name ....

Address ....

....

....

Telephone ....

Name ....

Address ....

....

....

Telephone ....

Name ....

Address ....

....

....

Telephone ....

G

Name ....

Address ....

....

....

Telephone ....

Name ....

Address ....

....

....

Telephone ....

Name ....

Address ....

....

....

Telephone ....

Name ....

Address ....

....

....

Telephone ....

Name ....

Address ....

....

....

Telephone ....

The Music of a Bygone Age by John Melhuish Strudwick

Name ....

Address ....

....

Telephone ....

Name ....

Address ....

....

Telephone ....

Name ....

Address ....

....

Telephone ....

Name ....

Address ....

....

Telephone ....

Name ....

Address ....

....

Telephone ....

Name ....

Address ....

....

....

Telephone ....

Name ....

Address ....

....

....

Telephone ....

Name ....

Address ....

....

....

Telephone ....

Name ....

Address ....

....

....

Telephone ....

Name ....

Address ....

....

....

Telephone ....

H

Name ....

Address ....

....

....

Telephone ....

Name ....

Address ....

....

....

Telephone ....

Name ....

Address ....

....

....

Telephone ....

Name ....

Address ....

....

....

Telephone ....

Name ....

Address ....

....

....

Telephone ....

Name ....

Address ....

....

....

Telephone ....

Name ....

Address ....

....

....

Telephone ....

Name ....

Address ....

....

....

Telephone ....

Name ....

Address ....

....

....

Telephone ....

Name ....

Address ....

....

....

Telephone ....

Proserpine by Dante Gabriel Rossetti

Name ....

Address ....

....

....

Telephone ....

Name ....

Address ....

....

....

Telephone ....

Name ....

Address ....

....

....

Telephone ....

Name ....

Address ....

....

....

Telephone ....

Name ....

Address ....

....

....

Telephone ....

J

Name ....

Address ....

....

Telephone ....

Name ....

Address ....

....

Telephone ....

Name ....

Address ....

....

Telephone ....

Name ....

Address ....

....

Telephone ....

Name ....

Address ....

....

Telephone ....

Name ....
Address ....
....
....
Telephone ....

Name ....
Address ....
....
....
Telephone ....

Name ....
Address ....
....
....
Telephone ....

Name ....
Address ....
....
....
Telephone ....

Name ....
Address ....
....
....
Telephone ....

J

Name ....

Address ....

....

Telephone ....

Name ....

Address ....

....

Telephone ....

Name ....

Address ....

....

Telephone ....

Name ....

Address ....

....

Telephone ....

Name ....

Address ....

....

Telephone ....

The Lady of Shalott (1888) by John William Waterhouse

J

Name ....

Address ....

....

Telephone ....

Name ....

Address ....

....

Telephone ....

Name ....

Address ....

....

Telephone ....

Name ....

Address ....

....

Telephone ....

Name ....

Address ....

....

Telephone ....

Name ....

Address ....

....

....

Telephone ....

Name ....

Address ....

....

....

Telephone ....

Name ....

Address ....

....

....

Telephone ....

Name ....

Address ....

....

....

Telephone ....

Name ....

Address ....

....

....

Telephone ....

K

Name ....

Address ....

....

Telephone ....

Name ....

Address ....

....

Telephone ....

Name ....

Address ....

....

Telephone ....

Name ....

Address ....

....

Telephone ....

Name ....

Address ....

....

Telephone ....

Name ....

Address ....

....

....

Telephone ....

Name ....

Address ....

....

....

Telephone ....

Name ....

Address ....

....

....

Telephone ....

Name ....

Address ....

....

....

Telephone ....

Name ....

Address ....

....

....

Telephone ....

The Child Enthroned by Thomas Cooper Gotch

Name ....

Address ....

....

....

Telephone ....

Name ....

Address ....

....

....

Telephone ....

Name ....

Address ....

....

....

Telephone ....

Name ....

Address ....

....

....

Telephone ....

Name ....

Address ....

....

....

Telephone ....

L

Name ....

Address ....

....

Telephone ....

Name ....

Address ....

....

Telephone ....

Name ....

Address ....

....

Telephone ....

Name ....

Address ....

....

Telephone ....

Name ....

Address ....

....

Telephone ....

Name ....

Address ....

....

....

Telephone ....

Name ....

Address ....

....

....

Telephone ....

Name ....

Address ....

....

....

Telephone ....

Name ....

Address ....

....

....

Telephone ....

Name ....

Address ....

....

....

Telephone ....

M

Name ....

Address ....

....

Telephone ....

Name ....

Address ....

....

Telephone ....

Name ....

Address ....

....

Telephone ....

Name ....

Address ....

....

Telephone ....

Name ....

Address ....

....

Telephone ....

Ophelia by John William Waterhouse

M

Name ....
Address ....
....
....
Telephone ....

Name ....
Address ....
....
....
Telephone ....

Name ....
Address ....
....
....
Telephone ....

Name ....
Address ....
....
....
Telephone ....

Name ....
Address ....
....
....
Telephone ....

Name

Address

Telephone

Name

Address

Telephone

Name

Address

Telephone

Name

Address

Telephone

Name

Address

Telephone

Name ....

Address ....

....

Telephone ....

Name ....

Address ....

....

Telephone ....

Name ....

Address ....

....

Telephone ....

Name ....

Address ....

....

Telephone ....

Name ....

Address ....

....

Telephone ....

Name ....

Address ....

....

....

Telephone ....

Name ....

Address ....

....

....

Telephone ....

Name ....

Address ....

....

....

Telephone ....

Name ....

Address ....

....

....

Telephone ....

Name ....

Address ....

....

....

Telephone ....

The Day Dream by Dante Gabriel Rossetti

Name ....

Address ....

....

....

Telephone ....

Name ....

Address ....

....

....

Telephone ....

Name ....

Address ....

....

....

Telephone ....

Name ....

Address ....

....

....

Telephone ....

Name ....

Address ....

....

....

Telephone ....

O

Name ....

Address ....

....

Telephone ....

Name ....

Address ....

....

Telephone ....

Name ....

Address ....

....

Telephone ....

Name ....

Address ....

....

Telephone ....

Name ....

Address ....

....

....

Telephone ....

Name ....

Address ....

....

....

Telephone ....

Name ....

Address ....

....

....

Telephone ....

Name ....

Address ....

....

....

Telephone ....

Name ....

Address ....

....

....

Telephone ....

Name ....

Address ....

....

....

Telephone ....

P

Name ....
Address ....
....
Telephone ....

Name ....
Address ....
....
Telephone ....

Name ....
Address ....
....
Telephone ....

Name ....
Address ....
....
Telephone ....

Name ....
Address ....
....
Telephone ....

'I am Half Sick of Shadows,' said the Lady of Shalott by Sidney Harold Meteyard

P

Name ....

Address ....

....

....

Telephone ....

Name ....

Address ....

....

Telephone ....

Name ....

Address ....

....

Telephone ....

Name ....

Address ....

....

Telephone ....

Name ....

Address ....

....

....

Telephone ....

Name

Address

Telephone

Name

Address

Telephone

Name

Address

Telephone

Name

Address

Telephone

Name

Address

Telephone

Q

Name

Address

Telephone

Name

Address

Telephone

Name

Address

Telephone

Name

Address

Telephone

Name

Address

Telephone

Name ....

Address ....

....

....

Telephone ....

Name ....

Address ....

....

....

Telephone ....

Name ....

Address ....

....

....

Telephone ....

Name ....

Address ....

....

....

Telephone ....

Name ....

Address ....

....

....

Telephone ....

The Bower Meadow by Dante Gabriel Rossetti

Name ....

Address ....

....

....

Telephone ....

Name ....

Address ....

....

....

Telephone ....

Name ....

Address ....

....

....

Telephone ....

Name ....

Address ....

....

....

Telephone ....

Name ....

Address ....

....

....

Telephone ....

R

Name ....

Address ....

....

....

Telephone ....

Name ....

Address ....

....

....

Telephone ....

Name ....

Address ....

....

....

Telephone ....

Name ....

Address ....

....

....

Telephone ....

Name ....

Address ....

....

....

Telephone ....

R

Name ....
Address ....
....
....
Telephone ....

Name ....
Address ....
....
....
Telephone ....

Name ....
Address ....
....
....
Telephone ....

Name ....
Address ....
....
....
Telephone ....

Name ....
Address ....
....
....
Telephone ....

S

Name ....

Address ....

....

....

Telephone ....

Name ....

Address ....

....

....

Telephone ....

Name ....

Address ....

....

....

Telephone ....

Name ....

Address ....

....

....

Telephone ....

Name ....

Address ....

....

....

Telephone ....

Madeline After Prayer by Daniel Maclise

S

Name ....

Address ....

....

....

Telephone ....

Name ....

Address ....

....

Telephone ....

Name ....

Address ....

....

Telephone ....

Name ....

Address ....

....

Telephone ....

Name ....

Address ....

....

Telephone ....

Name ....

Address ....

....

....

Telephone ....

Name ....

Address ....

....

....

Telephone ....

Name ....

Address ....

....

....

Telephone ....

Name ....

Address ....

....

....

Telephone ....

Name ....

Address ....

....

....

Telephone ....

$\mathcal{T}$

Name ....

Address ....

....

Telephone ....

Name ....

Address ....

....

Telephone ....

Name ....

Address ....

....

Telephone ....

Name ....

Address ....

....

Telephone ....

Name ....

Address ....

....

Telephone ....

Name ....

Address ....

....

....

Telephone ....

Name ....

Address ....

....

....

Telephone ....

Name ....

Address ....

....

....

Telephone ....

Name ....

Address ....

....

....

Telephone ....

Name ....

Address ....

....

....

Telephone ....

Mariana by Sir John Everett Millais

T

Name ....

Address ....

....

....

Telephone ....

Name ....

Address ....

....

....

Telephone ....

Name ....

Address ....

....

....

Telephone ....

Name ....

Address ....

....

....

Telephone ....

Name ....

Address ....

....

....

Telephone ....

$\mathcal{U}$

Name ....
Address ....
....
Telephone ....

Name ....
Address ....
....
Telephone ....

Name ....
Address ....
....
Telephone ....

Name ....
Address ....
....
Telephone ....

Name ....
Address ....
....
Telephone ....

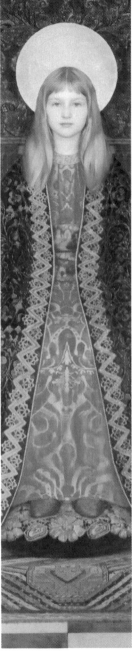

Name

Address

Telephone

Name

Address

Telephone

Name

Address

Telephone

Name

Address

Telephone

Name

Address

Telephone

𝒱

Name ....

Address ....

....

....

Telephone ....

Name ....

Address ....

....

....

Telephone ....

Name ....

Address ....

....

....

Telephone ....

Name ....

Address ....

....

....

Telephone ....

Name ....

Address ....

....

....

Telephone ....

Veronica Veronese by Dante Gabriel Rossetti

𝒱

Name ....

Address ....

....

....

Telephone ....

Name ....

Address ....

....

....

Telephone ....

Name ....

Address ....

....

....

Telephone ....

Name ....

Address ....

....

....

Telephone ....

Name ....

Address ....

....

....

Telephone ....

Name ....

Address ....

....

....

Telephone ....

Name ....

Address ....

....

....

Telephone ....

Name ....

Address ....

....

....

Telephone ....

Name ....

Address ....

....

....

Telephone ....

Name ....

Address ....

....

....

Telephone ....

W

Name ....

Address ....

....

....

Telephone ....

Name ....

Address ....

....

....

Telephone ....

Name ....

Address ....

....

....

Telephone ....

Name ....

Address ....

....

....

Telephone ....

Name ....

Address ....

....

....

Telephone ....

Name ....

Address ....

....

....

Telephone ....

Name ....

Address ....

....

....

Telephone ....

Name ....

Address ....

....

Telephone ....

Name ....

Address ....

....

....

Telephone ....

Name ....

Address ....

....

....

Telephone ....

X·Y·Z

Name ....

Address ....

....

Telephone ....

Name ....

Address ....

....

Telephone ....

Name ....

Address ....

....

Telephone ....

Name ....

Address ....

....

Telephone ....

Name ....

Address ....

....

Telephone ....

Name ....

Address ....

....

....

Telephone ....

Name ....

Address ....

....

....

Telephone ....

Name ....

Address ....

....

....

Telephone ....

Name ....

Address ....

....

....

Telephone ....

Name ....

Address ....

....

....

Telephone ....

Name

Address

Telephone

Name

Address

Telephone

Name

Address

Telephone

Name

Address

Telephone

Name

Address

Telephone